Otherworld, Underworld,
Prayer Porch

DAVID BOTTOMS

Otherworld, Underworld, Prayer Porch

Copper Canyon Press
Port Townsend, Washington

Cover art: Frank Hunter, *Pools of Light,* platinum/palladium print

Copper Canyon Press is in residence at Fort Worden State Park in Port Townsend, Washington, under the auspices of Centrum. Centrum is a gathering place for artists and creative thinkers from around the world, students of all ages and backgrounds, and audiences seeking extraordinary cultural enrichment.

LIBRARY OF CONGRESS CATALOGING-IN-PUBLICATION DATA

Names: Bottoms, David, author.

Title: Otherworld, underworld, prayer porch / David Bottoms.

Description: Port Townsend, Washington : Copper Canyon Press, 2018.

Identifiers: LCCN 2017031556 | ISBN 9781556595202 (pbk. : alk. paper) 9781556595363 (hardcover)

Classification: LCC PS3552.O819 A6 2018 | DDC 811/.54—dc23

LC record available at https://lccn.loc.gov /2017031556

9 8 7 6 5 4 3 2 FIRST PRINTING

Copper Canyon Press

Post Office Box 271

Port Townsend, Washington 98368

www.coppercanyonpress.org

This book, and everything else, is for Kelly and Rachel

ACKNOWLEDGMENTS

Poems in this book appeared originally in *Anglican Theological Review, Birmingham Poetry Review, The Cortland Review, The Georgia Review, The Hopkins Review, Kenyon Review, Literary Matters* (Association of Literary Scholars, Critics, and Writers), *New Republic, The New Yorker* ("Eye to Eye" and "Spring 2012"), *Plume, Rattle, Shenandoah, The Southern Review, The Yale Review,* and online at Poem-a-Day from the Academy of American Poets. Thanks to the editors of these magazines.

"Baptists" also appeared online in *Poetry Daily.*

"A Small Remembrance" appeared online as a *Shenandoah* featured poem with commentary by William Wright.

"Hubert Blankenship" appeared in *Best American Poetry 2016,* edited by Edward Hirsch.

Thanks to Edward Hirsch, Thomas Lux, Dave Smith, and Ernest Suarez for helpful readings of these poems.

Special thanks to Michael Wiegers and Copper Canyon Press.

Contents

4

5

Otherworld, Underworld,
Prayer Porch

1

Why, then, do I kneel still
striking my prayers on a stone
heart?

R.S. THOMAS

An Absence

Near the end, only one thing matters.

Yes, it has something to do with the moon and the way
the moon balances so nervously

on the ridge of the barn. This is the landscape of my childhood —
my grandfather's country store, his barn, his pasture.

His chicken houses are already falling, but near the end
only the one thing matters.

It has to do with the prudence of his woods,
the way the trembling needles prove the wind.

Let's sit here by the fence
and watch for the fox that comes each night to the pasture.

Imagine how the moon cools the water in the cow pond.
Yes, things happen in the cool white spaces,

those moments you turn your head —
the way the trembling branch suggests the owl,

or the print by the pond suggests the fox.
Near the end, though, only one thing matters,

and nothing, not even the fox, moves as quietly.

Studying the Small Hill

Sometimes when my wife and daughter are asleep
I stumble outside
with our dog at three or four in the morning to piss in the yard.
In winter the moon scorches the tree branches,
and in summer it frosts the hillside
with a shabby glaze.

Then the bird feeders standing in the smudged shadows
of the maples
look like human skulls impaled on poles —
and sometimes wind and crickets and tree frogs
make lurid voices in the trees.

This is when I empty myself of anger and resentment,
and listen to them puddle
in the grass at my feet.

Jack runs the fence line and trots out
of the shadows, panting, to piss in the grass beside me.
Often in his eyes there is more to envy
than anything human,
and gauging the frantic influence
of the moon, I study the small hill bleeding shadows.
It's easy then to affirm the Christ metaphor
and all the tenuous ways
tenderness seeps into the world.

Slow Nights in the Bass Boat

Some nights when the fishing slows,
when the stripers
and hybrids drift through the cove like elusive thoughts,
you crank in the jig, prop the rod in the boat.

Some nights the trees on the bank are black and soundless,
a fat wall of darkness,
and the silence on the water feels like the voice
of a great absence.

Across the wide cove the lights of the bait shop
flicker like insects,
and, finally, a few stars struggle through the shredded clouds.

Silence, then, exceeds the darkness. Silence.

You grasp the gunwales and lean forward,
you catch a long breath.
That gnawing in your chest sharpens and spreads.
Your grip tightens.

The rustle in your ear is something grand and awful
straining to announce itself.
Your jaw trembles. Out of your yearning
the silence shapes a name.

Question on Allatoona

The moon was in the sky and on the water at the same time, and the sky
filled with stars. A dock jutted into the cove,

and the banks were heavily wooded and dark, the whole cove sizzling
with small sounds. From out of the woods on the far bank,

an owl called twice, paused, then hooted again.
Beyond the cove the lake widened quickly,

and a mile or more away
lights of the fishing camp flickered on the surface of the lake.

Our tackle box sat closed on the floor of the boat.

Far behind us on the porch of a cabin, a guitar
backed up a mandolin. We listened

instead for the question with no answer,

watched the moon on the water, then the moon in the sky,
and when enough silence had passed,

the frogs let go in great bellows up and down
the edge of the water.

There were no bass in that cove. No lunkers,
not even the pretense of a fish. Nobody even bothered

to untangle the backlashed reel.

Photo: Captured Gator, Canton, Georgia, 1960

Every few years a small one
would nab a trotline or waddle out of a cove where a Boy Scout
was grilling burgers. Crowds then, and theories —
somebody's pet from Florida
flushed down a toilet or tossed into a creek.

Where I was raised anything unusual became a spectacle,
like this four-foot gator
held by Lee Spears behind the South Canton Trading Post.

Years later, in Florida, I paddled over
dozens of them in Lake Talquin, their eyes on the water
like small balls of moonlight.

Not one ever rose to the boat, or even stirred,
which makes me wonder now
why this one, jaws wired shut, keeps gnawing at me with its desperate eyes.

Blessings, Yellow Mountain

I could have killed the snake.
I had a pistol in my belt, a 9mm, a Smith & Wesson,
accurate, deadly, and I was a good shot.

I could have easily killed the snake.

But Jack and I were walking his turf, walking federal land,
and he coiled so placidly
across the oak root, not even lifting his head
to acknowledge our passing.

I could have killed him with one shot. Nobody
would've heard. We were miles
from the nearest road.
But Jack wasn't even curious, and kept pulling me
up the path, sniffing the ground, lifting
a leg to piss on a stone.

I studied the moccasin for a moment longer —
the fat and terrible muscle of him, his black scales rippling
while a small wind
brushed his back with shadows.

Beautiful, sure, but I thought better of inching closer,
then followed the tug of Jack's leash.
Over the top of the ridge
sunlight sliced in layers through the trees,
and suddenly out of the branch quiver,
an antler moved.

2

We look at the world once,
    in childhood.
The rest is memory.

LOUISE GLÜCK

Spooked

If they spooked my old man he didn't show it,

only lifted me onto his shoulders and leaned against our back gate.
We stared across the woods,
the cornstalks rising out of our neighbor's garden.

Nobody knew what they were — those colored balls of light circling
the radio tower — a red ball, I remember, vaporous,

almost translucent, and a green and a blue, floating clockwise
around the tower.

My aunt had phoned in the middle of the night
to urge us into the yard for a look.

This was the summer of UFO reports, but if they spooked my old man,
he didn't show it.

At eight or nine I was already in a panic —
everything seemed a sign.

Oddly, though, no one ever mentioned that night again,
and how reliable, really, is the memory?

Now when I try to force my mind back, it runs straight
to the bulbs on a tree, those Christmas lights

glazing our dining-room windows.

The Grocer's Tackle Box

Not all dreams need to be realized.
PATTI SMITH

My obsession with gear
comes from a grandpa who rarely caught a fish

but kept in his tackle box one of every lure
he ever sold in his store.

I was especially drawn to the potbellied Bombers,
deep runners meant for pike and walleye,

but also the rainbow Rattlebugs, the pink doll flies trailing
yellow boas
loved by crappie and bass,

and the speckled plastic worms,
rubber frogs and tadpoles, the fat, tangerine Hula Poppers.

He kept his tackle box behind his cash register, tucked
behind cartons of bills and tax receipts.

As a boy I could walk by the Coke box and feel its draw.

Someday, he kept saying, he'd take me fishing
but never did. That was okay.

To prove the promise sometimes outweighs the fish,

he'd often let me open that box and thumb
the barbs on those lures.

My Old Man's Homemade Dagger

In a battered desk in the feed room of my grandfather's store,
I came across a knife
my father had made — high school, I'm guessing,
metal shop — a dagger with a bone handle,
blade cut from a metal file.

It looked ugly, dangerous.

"Put that back," he told me
when I brought it into the store. He hardly glanced
at the two-edged blade, good only for murder.

I was young, obedient. I put it back
but have held it for years in my memory,
just as he must've held it
in that desk drawer of rusted sockets and wrenches —

ugly, yes, but one of those things
so well made we could hardly let it go.

A Panic of Bats

Near evening I carry a folding chair into the plush shade
of the secret place
and sit facing the house

and the bat box hanging from the guest-room gable.

A quiet breeze in the leaf shelter
as they rise from the box and flit like ashes out of a bonfire,
black, black, black, rising

and flitting like ashes. My gaze flies
with them across the fence
and over the side yard, the way I followed, years ago, the ashes

of a burning house, little black wings drifting
over the wavy panic
of children crowding an upstairs window,

drifting across the hillside, rising and rising, falling
and falling and falling
onto the backs of grazing horses,
into the tall grass of my grandfather's pasture.

Summer 1968

We'd watch the news on my portable Philco.
The jungle was black and white. The bodies were black and white.

The whole house strained in its silence. I was 1-A.

One night my old man threw an alarm clock across my room.
He screamed something, but all I caught

was a cheap alarm clock, the size of a softball, ringing in the wallboard.

The screen flickered. The jungle snowed gray, the bodies gray.
The alarm clock, stuck in the wallboard, rang

for a minute or more. Nobody touched it for days.

Baptists

At Canton First Baptist no one ever spoke of mythologies or metaphor.
No one in the pulpit, huffing and red-faced,

ever asked why the prophets had long drifted into dust and silence.

Desert was simply a wilderness of sand. Blood was blood,
water was wine,

and wine (grape juice) was sometimes blood.

Most Sundays my mind was someplace else entirely, racing
the engine of my father's Impala, or breaking

a curveball over home plate, or casting

a lure over choir loft and organ, over stained-glass disciples
and net-draped fishing boats, struggling

to hook a thought, to reel it to the surface, clean, untangled,

without snagging the pulpit
or the back of a pew.

Bring the Beautiful Horses

Some days nothing helps.

Some days not even a basket of apples will bring the black horses
out of the past,

and Christ Pantocrator
seems little more than the face of an absurd hippie.

(My old man bent toward the gaping mouth. He sniffed, it was confirmed.
Nothing would help.)

Some days the sweetest words will not bring a blessing from the sky,
or sweeten the breakfast table with a smile,

or bring the beautiful horses out of the magical past.

(Nobody knew death like my father —
the Solomons, Wake Island, Guadalcanal. Thirty years

prepping bodies in a funeral home.) Some days on the prayer porch
the petitions never clear the trees,

and there is nothing to do but rock
and watch the wind rattle the maples and pin oaks.

(When he turned toward my aunt and shook his head,
everyone knew it was accomplished.)

Some days those beautiful horses will not leave the shadows
of their hill.

Some days nothing helps.

Turkey Shoot, 1961

No one actually shot a turkey. Only targets strung across a wire
at the end of our practice field.

Shotguns only. A dollar a shot (benefiting the local Little League),
and the closest pellet to the center of the target

won a ticket for a turkey at the local Kroger.
So mostly luck, though a big-bore gun increased your odds.

My slow cousin breeched a double-barreled 12-gauge,
dropped in a shell, and stepped to the line.

Startling blast, turf flying up at his feet!

He turned, amazed, to face the crowd, his stunned eyes asking
the saddest question.

(What did they say
about that moment of obvious embarrassment,

my father's muffled sigh, my uncle's grim face?)

After the special classes, the schoolyard teasing, the rage,
the tears, confusion, and clumsiness —

everything gone so wrong so early — how could this boy
in morning fog and powder drift

grow to become
what my mother called *the sweetest man alive*?

Hubert Blankenship

Needing credit, he edges through the heavy door, head down,
and quietly closes the screen behind him.

This is Blankenship, father of five, owner of a plow horse and a cow.

Out of habit he leans against the counter by the stove.
He pats the pockets of his overalls

for the grocery list penciled on a torn paper bag,
then rolls into a strip of newsprint

the last of his Prince Albert.
He hardly takes his eyes off his boot, sliced on one side

to accommodate his bunion, and hands
the list to my grandfather. Bull of the Woods, three tins

of sardines, Spam, peanut butter, two loaves of bread (Colonial),
then back to the musty feed room

where he ignores the hand truck leaning against the wall

and hefts onto his shoulder a hundred-pound bag of horse feed.
He rises to full height, snorting

but hardly burdened,
and parades, head high, to the bed of his pickup.

Foul Ball

The river was off-limits, but occasionally a foul ball would fly back

over the press box, over the narrow drive
and down the hill,

and there we were — where what we called the ballpark rock
jutted into the Etowah.

On hot nights the stench would make you gag.

Two miles below the rendering plant
and chicken parts still flooded up in the pool beyond the rock —
clots of dirty feathers, feet,

an occasional head with glazed eyes wide.
We'd hold our noses and try to breathe through our mouths.

Once, though, the smell was too much
and we had to give it up.

Listen, it wasn't what you think. It was only Little League,
and they gave you free ice cream

for retrieving a foul. No, we weren't overcome
by thoughts of filth, disease,
or fish kills. We were running down a long hill, dodging

trees and undergrowth, trying
to find a ball before it found the river.

Black Horses

Just past Ledbetter's Grocery, on our shortcut
to the Pony League ballpark, you could cut your eyes quickly

to the right and catch two black horses

grazing a weedy field. In sunlight
a rickety barn leaned far behind them, near the woods,

and a barbwire fence ran slack along the road.
In starlight, darkness surrounded

their eyes, the white blazes of their foreheads,
and the fence became black

and barbed with diamonds. They were always there,
grazing, taken for granted.

(Isn't memory often about loneliness?)

Years, though, since I've recalled
those horses I rarely noticed on my way to ball games.

(Yes, it's true, they remind me of my father,

his wingtips dusting up a coach's box.)
Now even the landscape is changed — the road closed off,

the highway widened,
the pasture graded, graveled, and paved —

so what does it mean
that they still graze that field parching behind my eyes?

A Nervous Boy

1

I was a nervous boy, small and nervous.
I liked to hide.

I sought out places of refuge —
close spaces where thick air was a balm for remorse.

And there were many secret places
between the store and the dog lots, the barn and ball field.

The chicken house, for instance, at the top of the path
to my grandfather's dog lots,
empty for years
but still rich with the smell of broilers and feed —

a quiet dark enjoyed by rats
and rat snakes, spiders, roaches, beetles, earwigs,

and once, a stray dog birthing her litter in the dank sawdust.

One day I hid there all afternoon.

2

I hadn't wanted to shoot the rabbit.
It sat on a ridge of the pasture, stiff ears reaching for the sky,

and even from that distance I could see it trembling.
Wind whipped the grass and blew in
the stench of dog turds. My stomach turned.

My grandfather laid the barrel of his rifle on a fence rail
and held the stock to my shoulder.
I was a good shot. I sighted the head, I steadied,

but I didn't want to shoot that rabbit trembling
in perpetual surrender. I inched high, squeezed, and dirt flew up
a foot beyond it.

My grandfather sighed as though my failure
suggested the sort of man I'd be.
But I didn't want to shoot that rabbit.

He shrugged. He shook his head.
He pumped the rifle again
and pressed the stock tight against my shoulder.

   3
From the chicken house
I could hear the horse neighing in his stall,
the crows in the pines on the hill above the dog lots.

After a while, shouts rose from the ball field at the foot of the hill.
But I only wanted to hide.

I only wanted the dark, the solitude.

I don't recall the shot or the rabbit jumping
sideways and falling,
only that old man lifting it by the ears

and flinging it into the dog lot.
I must've shot the rabbit.

A Small Remembrance

I have learned the impossibility of avoiding surrender.
ANDRE DUBUS

1

Beside a Coleman tent,
beside a lake, I light a small fire of damp sticks and twigs.

The flames struggle to catch in the kindling.
Smoke billows and blows away.

Across the lake a coyote wails (or a stray dog).
Then wind again in the trees.

A doctor I knew once
told me that every time he watched a patient die
he thought he could see something tangible

leaving the body. He didn't say soul,
but I knew what he meant.

Surely the soul billows and blows away.

Tonight I light a small fire
of remembrance, a small fire by a still lake,
in a light drizzle. The month is November,
though the night isn't cold.

Smoke billows and blows away.

Memory also, I fear,
the features of a face, the sound of a voice,
a typical phrase.

2

When I can't reach my daughter, or my wife,
and the black flower
of anxiety blooms in my chest and chokes off my breath,

I try to think of my father, years ago, away at war
in the oily water of the Pacific,
the black jungles of Florida Island and Guadalcanal.

I try to imagine the darkness blooming
in the chest of his father,
his mother on her prayer bones at bedside,

their anxiety as they hover over their radio, twisting dials,
desperate for war news,

the static of radio, wind, and whispered plea,
which makes my worry small.

3

Some mornings on the prayer porch
with the brown eyes of Christ Pantocrator gazing at me
from Kelly's icon,

I pray for the coyote den in the woods
beyond the cul-de-sac.

I pray to be like the coyote, wary and full of craft,
fully aware of the moment
and only the moment,

praying urgently to the moon and the trees
and the steel wind hacking through the scrub brush.

Who wouldn't want to know what she knows?
That is, what she knows
and nothing more?

4

Landscapes plowed over, paved over, prayed over,
live only in memory.

My grandfather's house and grocery,
his field and barn, our house of green shingles beside

the highway, the homemade infield
where my old man hit grounders and taught the subtleties
of the double play —

how many memories are left
for them to live in? If I stand in that Kmart parking lot, trying
to take bearings — the store must have sat here,

my grandfather's house there,
the barn behind me (somewhere), our house

down the highway — no dice.
The pasture graded and paved, lined with paint for parking cars,

all's a vague approximation.

5

Clouds roll and the rain picks up.
The lake is black.
I squint and gaze back years across the black water.

A spotlight beams out of the darkness and strikes
the superstructure of the ship.

Six gun turrets swivel to shoot it out.

Soon barrels flash all across the horizon —
thunder and fire —

the water itself on fire.

In the lifeboat someone asked
about the pain.
                    (Only his right hand
kept his intestines from spilling into the boat.)

A little sting, he said, from the salt water.

    6
I remember my grandmother's cedar chest,
the rich smell of the kept
and sacred —

crocheted bedspread folded in plastic, hand-stitched quilts,
the wooden box of battle ribbons, the purple cameo
shaped like a heart.

The profile out of history.

A small boy shouldn't be trusted with such things.

    7
Beside this cabin tent,
beside this lake, I light a small fire of damp sticks and twigs.

Clouds shred. Smoke billows slightly
and blows away. The coyote (or stray dog)
prays loudly to the moon.

The breath tries to catch in my chest.

Who survived two years
in a San Diego hospital came home to leave
many memories,
though the soul will finally billow and blow away.

And memory.

Smoke off a damp fire.

Cathedrals

1

Near nightfall, in summer, an owl would plague the scrub woods
beyond Cantrell's pond.

Or a mourning dove, hard to tell. (Question or lament,
question or lament?)

Branches slapped the roof and sides of the tree house.
Light fell
in thin slices through the oak

and dimmed away in the shadows. The woods beyond the pond
dimmed away, then the pond,
then the yard.
            Spiders took to their corners,
roaches to their corners. Traffic thinned slowly on the highway.

Then the screech owl would startle the scrub woods.

Soon someone else would call, someone from the house.
But I'd not answer. Not yet. I liked to hide.
I liked to sit alone in the dark.

No one knew where to find me. Still,
if I held my breath for a moment, if I stayed quiet, if I listened
and didn't breathe,

a wind might rise and garble my name.

2

You could hardly breathe.

In a corner of the hayloft, where a thin ray of light
from a grimy window fell once a day
in midafternoon

and drew across the loft a quivering veil of dust,
you became almost breathless.

Behind a few tattered hay bales
and moldy bags of oats,
you could, in those days, feel a credible silence.
(Careful, though! The feed chutes!)

One Sunday, when I was a boy,
my uncle took me there and draped his jacket
across a sturdy bale.

We used it as a pew, and the prayer he spoke rose
and faded into the rafters.
He lifted a finger to his lips, as if to say *Listen.*

(Silence is the language of faith.) Suddenly, at that sign,

no whistling through windows
of horse stalls, no rasping of floorboards, no worry
of crossbeams propping up rafters and roof.

3

A deep green cave of branches. A leafy darkness.
Something waiting to be born?

I'd sit beside the trunk and gaze up. On clear days patches
of blue ragged
through the upper branches. (Enough to make a sailor's suit?)

In a light rain the green leaves sparkled,
and once I found a glossy snake skin draped
in a low fork.

But at Christmas the branches sparkled with electric bulbs —
red, green, and blue
and the yellow of traffic lights. My father climbed a ladder
and strung them all the way to the top.

Taller than the house, with leaves as wide
as a small boy's head, cones
as large as footballs.

I was a small, nervous boy.
I liked to hide
and nurture my prayers in dusty places.

Under the skirts
of my grandmother's magnolia, a gentleness set in.

A gentleness
is all I knew to call it, a calm, a solitude.

3

See how the past is not finished
here in the present

W.S. MERWIN

Hospital

He didn't want to go to the hospital.

He didn't want to shoot anyone, but he didn't want to go
to the hospital.

He held the pistol, cocked, on the two ambulance men
and cursed them,
though cursing wasn't like him. He trembled

and wept when my mother talked the pistol out of his hands.
An old man again, he lay back on the bed
and trembled and wept.

They phoned me at work, asking
what they should do. When you're fifty miles away

it's hard to know what's right or wrong.
His ankle was swollen. My mother feared a blood clot.

He didn't care, he'd had enough of hospitals.
Pain must have shot back

across the years — Japanese searchlight
across black water, shell-blast in gun turret, fire on water.

They lifted him from the lifeboat onto a gurney
and drove him to the hospital.

Two days later, he died.

Dress Blues

Bad luck, he believed, to throw away a Bible. So a small stack
moldered on a table in the basement—

a pocket New Testament with Psalms and Proverbs, a gilded King James
in a red leather jacket, an Oxford Revised Standard,

a Tyndale's New Testament. (Where did he get that?)
I walked down one morning to find his leather-bound Masonic

at the bottom of the stack,
which brought back those evenings

he'd come home late, his jacket smelling of stale tobacco,
and on his breath a sweetness

it took me years to recognize. What mysteries were revealed
those late nights in the windowless lodge

he never revealed to me. At his funeral the Grand Master stood
at the grave and challenged us

to change our lives. (Someday we'd be lying in his place.)
Two sailors in dress blues

folded the flag that had covered the casket
while a third stood off and bugled taps — solemn, mournful, lovely.

Weeks later, I learned it was a recording,
but still recalled
that glint of sunlight as the bugle touched his lips.

Hovering

When the Grand Master
of the local lodge stood beside my father's grave,
he didn't preach to my mother,
or to me, or to the dozen or so nephews, nieces, and cousins gathered
under the funeral-home tent.

No, he spoke to the treetops edging the cemetery
and to the gray clouds shredding over the long valley of graves.

This must be, he said, the beginning of the letting go.

My biggest problem has always been letting go.
Sometimes I'll text my daughter twelve, maybe fifteen, times a day.
All I want
is to know she's safe.

But it annoys her.

When you're twenty-one, you're easily annoyed.
And, let's face it, I hover.

On the prayer porch my words rise
through the screen and over the trees lining the backyard.

I pray for safety, knowing there is no safety,
only a short deferment,
                          then that Bible rises again
under the funeral-home tent,
a wind ripples through distant trees
and low clouds shred over the dark valley.

Eye to Eye

Suddenly I noticed the silence — the robins, jays, mockingbirds
all gone quiet, the cardinals and song sparrows quiet.

Then as Jack and I turned onto the homeward loop of our walk,
the sky startled us with a shriek —

two hawks circling above the pines, screaming from tree to tree,
two hawks from the heavy nest

above our neighbor's house, screaming then going silent
in the branches of a Bradford pear.

We crossed under that tree and stopped to catch
the larger hawk, the female, eye to eye.

Jack sat by the curb and stared. I stared.
And head cocked, leaning forward, she stared, incredulous,

working her jaw, quietly, nervously.
I made faces, snarled, bared my teeth, and the hawk

never flinched. Only stared until those orange inflamed eyes
became the terrible jaundiced eyes of my father

that final moment he raised his lids.
(The silenced voice tells the truth.)

Like my father's jaw, her jaw trembled.

Spring 2012

I rub my eyes. The world is still green —
a lime dust coating the porch tiles, rocking chairs, patio, yard,

delicate as a mourning veil.

A green finch dances between the bird feeders.
I can't breathe, my eyes water. My friend can't breathe either.

She's lost her son to an IED. No details yet. Routine patrol
around a dusty village far away.

Tea waits on the table between us, and two blueberry scones.
Impossible, of course, to talk about loneliness

or vague aspirations. Rain today, then a cooling.
In a week or so, dogwoods flowering along the back fence.

After that, maple sap staining the hoods of our cars.

Attic Rats

Squirrels (or rats) were keeping us awake, a constant scratching
in the attic and walls, tag among the rafters.

I was afraid they'd start a fire, chew the insulation off the wiring,
so climbed up the garage ladder

to spray some Deer Off, at least keep them away
from the furnace.

When my foot missed a joist and my leg plunged
through the ceiling

I didn't need my screaming wife to tell me something
had gone wrong. Yes,

something had betrayed me, had gone south,
and I remembered my old man

looking up from his bed at Cherokee Northside,
his toothless gaping mouth,

the stunned look in his jaundiced eyes. I swept up
the spilled insulation. (Littered with rat pellets.)

I patched the hole with cardboard, vowed to call a handyman.

For weeks I've lived with that patch,
that gasping shock.

Staying in Touch

When my friend's brother shot himself, she charged his cellphone,
and just before they closed the coffin, slipped it
into the pocket of his suit.

He was rarely without it. Even the pastor
who did the eulogy praised
                          his gift for being in touch.

Twice at graveside a ringer went off
and people struggled
with umbrellas and raincoats
to pull hushed phones from pockets and handbags.

Only his sister stood frozen under the funeral-home tent.

Weeks passed as she sent to his cell her daily text.
No response, of course.
                    It was only a gesture,
and after a while she stopped checking for missed messages.

The rains stopped also. Summer brought drought.

It was always a gesture, of course. No answers
would be forthcoming. Even she knew
there would be other business

to attend,
and after a few restless days the charge would die.

Kelly Sleeping

Sometimes when she sleeps, her face against the pillow (or sheet)
almost achieves an otherworldly peace.

Sometimes when the traffic and bother of the day dissolve
and her deeper self eases out, when sunlight edges

through curtains and drapes the bed, I know she's in another place,
a purer place, which perhaps doesn't include me,

though certainly includes love, which may include the possibility of me.
Sometimes then her face against the sheet (or pillow)

achieves (almost) an otherworldly calm (do I dare say that?)
and glows (almost) as it glowed years ago

just after our daughter's head slipped through the birth canal.

I remember that wet sticky swirl of hair
turning slightly so the slick body might follow more easily,

and how the midwife or nurse or doctor (or someone)
laid a firm open hand under that head

and guided our child into the world.
When that hand laid our daughter on her mother's breast,

such a sigh followed, a long

exhausted breath, and (stunned) I saw in my wife's face
an ecstasy I knew I'd never (quite) see again.

Remembering Flowers

I didn't know I loved flowers.
NAZIM HIKMET

Suddenly I considered lilies.
I'd never planted flowers, the soil in the yard too poor,

and me with no talent for nurturing.
But in that room where the paper robe, pale as a lily,

did nothing for the chill,
I remembered my grandmother on her prayer bones

in her flower bed, crumbling potting soil
through her grimy fingers

that some fresh bud might crop up from that mire.
And it did, I suppose, though I never gave

a petal of a flower a second glance.
But suddenly in that room of needles and charts

I whispered *hollyhock, dianthus, Helenium.*
Where did those words come from?

I knew nothing about flowers.
And, as though everything were still possible,

I remembered a flower bed and a woman on her knees,

and resolved to stop for seeds —
daisies, buttercups, delphiniums, lilies...

An Old Enemy

Just past midnight when I walked out back to piss in the yard

I saw at my feet
in a patch of moonlight

the old enemy coiled on the root of a cherry tree.

It didn't rattle or move, and I thought it might be dead,
then the fat tail twitched
as a slight wind washed the root with shadows.

I backed away slowly, looking for the shovel
I kept leaning against the fence.

It wasn't there. So thinking *omen,* I left the snake
and walked back into the house.

This morning I saw my mistake. A rope the tree trimmers
left last week
lay draped across the root of the cherry.

Omen? Maybe. But no mistake.

In deep memory the danger remains —
the fat rope
coiled and ready to strike.

Little King Snake on the Prayer Porch

Wanting to live, it had wedged itself between a porch rail
and the screen and hung there

as Jack barked and backed up and lunged forward
and barked again.

An Eastern king snake, jelly-black
with buttery stripes. Beautiful, yes, but slightly common.

Harmless, basically, a constrictor
good for eating rats and other vermin, also an eater

of rattlesnakes and moccasins.
Benevolent, basically,

though it tried to bite when I raked it with a stick.
I steered it toward the door

and watched it sidle across the grass
and thought of a time I would have taken more joy

in its appearance, would have felt it
to be something miraculous,

a necklace, say, fallen from a witch's neck,
suddenly come alive

and slithering into the brush.

All Beggars Would Ride

for Jane Hirshfield

Last night the beautiful horses of my boyhood galloped again

into my dream. I especially love the sleek black mare
with the white star between her eyes,

and remember her grace as she'd trot
across the pasture when I stretched my arm over the fence —

corn husks, an apple core, such small things, such large joy.
I've often wished I had a heart like that.

Ah, says my mother-in-law, *if wishes were horses. . .*

4

Now it is autumn and the
falling fruit

D.H. LAWRENCE

Sundown Syndrome

The last night my mother spent in Kennestone Hospital
my cell rang at four,
her voice raw and pleading — the nurses were trying to kill her,
I needed to phone the police.

Around that voice my bedroom tilted.

Nurses were wheeling everyone into the basement.
Thus all those hysterical gurneys clacking
down the hall. Nothing would convince her otherwise —

watch the elevators, listen
to the screams. No one damned to the basement
ever comes back.

Last evening, fifty geese circled chaotically
above our backyard pines, then vaguely fell into a V
to break up and flag again.

Something had gone haywire,
shorted-out in the nervous circuitry
of the world — dozens of Canada geese reeling

over the suburb, tumbling, wheeling, ragging-out
in a Babel of figure eights. A full two minutes
before the planet leveled

and sharp black lines
arrowed south over pine tops not quite dark.

My Mother's Abscess

The receptionist, in her marbled booth, jabs a pink nail into the phone.
All day, maybe, she hasn't noticed the potted ficus
between the revolving doors.

The potted ficus! Maybe no one has noticed but me
with my brown-bagged Dewar's and my fat Russian novel, on my way
to the second-floor waiting room
where, a few rooms down, surgeons are slicing a loop
from my mother's colon.

A snake in the ficus tree? Sure, as though it had slithered
out of some patient's dream, a red snake curled
like a bowel around the ficus, little red snake like something
out of a trick shop, curled
around the skinny trunk of the ficus.

When I was a kid I saw omens everywhere — a crow on the mailbox,
a black cat at a ball game, that evil number
turning up on Fridays...
                                        I scratch my beard.
Upstairs my mother lies drugged, beyond dreams, beyond signs,
and here I'm spooked by the tiniest snake?

A few leaves tremble, the body loops. The lewd head rises
like a little chip off the original nightmare.

Rehab

In 308 my mother is stewing. Not because a nurse smashed
her porcelain vase and scattered roses across the floor,

or because an aide swiped an apple salvaged from her lunch tray.

Even now from this bed, she feels dust invading her house,
glazing her china cabinet, wind whistling

under the plate-glass door in the den. The chill circles her kitchen.

The furnace is off, the house trembling. The bony clock creaks
in the shifting corner. Leaves swirl in the garage.

In 308 my mother broods, her cracked ribs are slow to mend.

She lies on her back, hands at her side, jaw set,
staring at the ceiling, at the blistered ceiling,

as though what she studies

are answers written in secret code
and not just water stains under a light fixture.

Baptist Women

My mother loves to talk about her health — in eighty-six years

seven major surgeries, two fractured hips,
five ribs, one ankle, assorted broken fingers and toes.

The church ladies who visit
don't seem to mind. They have their own maladies.

Outside the planet heats up, though it's not yet summer.
Squirrels thunder all afternoon on the roof.

My mother says something about the voice of God
rumbling in her hearing aid.

She also heard it two weeks ago, a wave in the static
of the emergency room — drip, hum, drip, hum.

A Baptist lady unwraps a casserole.

My mother loves to talk about her heart.
The church ladies who visit don't seem to mind.

They have their own maladies, or relatives who have them.
All saints suffer. It's common knowledge.

Arrival at Riverstone

Only a sparrow, she said. But I thought its song was lovely.

Then we went inside. People greeted us
and smiled, but none was my father. You could see

that in her face. Strangers all.
They shuffled behind walkers and canes, pointing

out the dining hall, the craft hall, the oversize flat-screen
for weekend movies. We trudged down the corridor

past the rec room where an old man leaning on a pool table
used his cane as a cue. Room 515. Last on the left.

Her name was misspelled on the door. She grumbled in.

Her bed was there, a dresser, two tables, her TV attached
to the cable, a few photos hung "to warm things up."

This place is full of old people, she said.
"A short period of adjustment is not uncommon,"

meaning nothing would be quite as it should.
The place was hot. I crossed the room to crack the window.

Ten feet away a small nest balanced
in the limbs of a dogwood. All she had to do was look.

Young Nurse, VA Hospital, 1945

Innocence, perhaps,
caused her to gasp and hold that memory for seventy years:

her leaning against the desk at the nurses' station,
going over meds
with the head nurse,

then a young sailor rolling up in a wheelchair.
Can they give him something
for his pain? His legs and feet are killing him.

She looks down at his scarred face,
his narrow shoulders wrapped in a khaki shawl,
his hands folded in his lap, then...

But I always knew what was coming, even the first time
I heard the story. Her grimace tipped me off.

And each time the story was repeated —
often three times in one visit —

I chalked it up to senility.

Now looking over the house
with only a stick or two of mildewed furniture,
the sagging deck, the ragged yard,
the downed fence,

I see that story clearly as an explanation —

the two bandaged stumps
a warning against the pain of absence.

The Moon My Mother Shot For

She aspired. Yes, she aspired.

But where in Canton, Georgia, could she wear the full-length mink
and the two-carat diamond she scraped

for twenty years to buy? Society
gathered at the country club and pool, the nine-hole golf course.

(My father, neither lawyer nor doctor, never played golf.)

And the twelve settings
of crystal that gathered dust for years in her china cabinet?

No one ever ate sherbet at our house.

All those lovely nights
when the full moon hung like a ballroom chandelier

over the used-car lot across the highway, that mink hung
wrapped in a sheet in their bedroom closet

and the diamond dulled quietly in its velvet box
in a vault at the Etowah Bank.

5

One must make a little prayer
from time to time.

I talk to God but the sky
is empty.

SYLVIA PLATH

Close Call

How fragile we are, between the few good moments.
JANE HIRSHFIELD

Starting the morning
on the prayer porch doesn't always ensure a calm day.

Like the Sunday I slipped on the rain-slick drive
and took nine stitches above my eye.

A wind draws the scent of lilacs across the yard,
pine needles rustle. The wound, though healed, still throbs.

Once again, I open my heart to Kelly's icon,
Christ Pantocrator hanging between two panels of screen.

My mother would call that face an idol. Most Baptists would.
But those calm eyes, that delicate hand blessing the world!

I open my heart again to the icon.
(Silence doesn't always mean absence.)

The rocker creaks rhythmically on the tile stones.

Maybe a Little Music

for Mike Mattison

Clearly the door to old age has opened.

Turns out it's the door to the prayer porch, swung wide, inviting me
to the rocking chair, the ceiling fan,

Christ Pantocrator hanging from his post between
panels of porch screen. Nothing to do here

but wait for something to happen. Somewhere else, most likely.
(When my old man lost his job

he went to bed and never got up.) Bird feeders empty
and nattering blue jays wondering

why the buffet's closed. Off in the neighborhood the growl
of leaf blowers and chain saw. Somewhere

a yard fanatic is butchering another tree.
This is what they call the blues, sans guitar and mouth harp.

Maybe a little music would help.

What to do but walk through the door and wait?

No Voice in the Trees

Tonight on the prayer porch, gloom veils the face
of Kelly's icon. Still, Christ Pantocrator

gazes calmly from the shadows. Out near the fence the cherry trees
cast a blue canopy over the secret place.

Jack roams the dark yard, pawing the shadows,
head hung low, sniffing for prowlers — chipmunks, rats, anything alive.

Wind brushes the cherry branches and suddenly I'm sitting
quietly with my father

who loved to rock at night on his backyard deck and listen
to the wind sweep his oaks. (Whose voice

in those trees?) How long now since he entered the ground
        and the silence,

the flat and stoneless ground, the ground kept smooth for mowing,
silent and treeless,

no voice within earshot?

Otherworld, Underworld, Prayer Porch

Maybe I'll rise from the dead.

Or live as a shadow. Or maybe I'll never leave you. At Emeritus
an old man plowing the hallway

with a three-wheeled walker
stopped me and grinned, *My goal is to live forever — so far, so good.*

Maybe we never get enough birdsong,
or watery soup
and over-steamed veggies. Still, from the prayer porch
eternity sometimes looks like a raw deal.

Eternal leaf blower and Weedwacker?

(A few days before he died my old man asked about the yard.)
Mostly blue jays at the feeder this morning, rude

and rowdy, and a few cardinals dripping off the trees
like the bloody tears of Christ.

Maybe we rise again only to the good things — honeysuckle,
robins, mockingbirds, doves,
fireflies toward evening, and along the back fence

the steady harping of tree frogs.
On the prayer porch, among the icons, such fancy notions.

Other Evidence

Rain now, heavy, and in a few hours
an icy mix, then snow after sundown, heavy, with gusting winds.

The weather guys are rarely wrong.

No milk on the grocery shelves, no bread,
no cornflakes. Certainly I'll regret not splitting more firewood.

Atlanta at a standstill — big rigs abandoned
on the interstate, cars spun out on the shoulders of the roads,

men and women trudging in the snow.

For years now
I've feared the tall pine leaning toward the house,

the loosening soil and the loud crash through the roof.
In the morning, sure, a kind of beauty —

the white blanket draping the yard,
Jack chasing the apple core I throw into the woods,

but also those strange tracks crossing
the yard, skirting the windows

and fading again into the trees.

A Scrawny Fox

Near the end, only one thing matters.

Yes, it has something to do with the moon and the way
the moon balances so nervously

on the rooftops of neighborhood houses. You remember the landscape
of your childhood, your house and yard,

the yards and houses of your friends. Near the end, though,
only one thing matters.

Maybe there was a wood where you played,
and that wood is gone now, paved over for parking cars.

At night, before sleep, it comes to you again —
your longing for the wilderness, the fox you saw last week

at the end of your cul-de-sac. Maybe you put out dog chow
and wait, at night, on your back porch.

Maybe you tire and close your eyes. Things happen
when you close your eyes — an owl leaves a branch trembling,

the dog food disappears. You'd love to see that fox again.
Near the end, though, only one thing matters,

and nothing, not even the fox, moves as quietly.

About the Author

David Bottoms is the author of ten books of poems, two novels, and a book of essays and interviews. Among the many awards he has received for his poetry are the Walt Whitman Award of the Academy of American Poets, an Ingram Merrill Award, an Award in Literature from the American Academy and Institute of Arts and Letters, the Levinson Prize and the Frederick Bock Prize from *Poetry,* and fellowships from the National Endowment for the Arts and the Guggenheim Foundation. He teaches at Georgia State University in Atlanta where he holds the John B. and Elena Diaz-Verson Amos Distinguished Chair in English Letters. He is a recipient of a Governor's Award for the Arts from Georgia Humanities, and he served for twelve years as Poet Laureate of Georgia.

Poetry is vital to language and living. Since 1972, Copper Canyon Press has published extraordinary poetry from around the world to engage the imaginations and intellects of readers, writers, booksellers, librarians, teachers, students, and donors.

WE ARE GRATEFUL FOR THE MAJOR SUPPORT PROVIDED BY:

THE PAUL G. ALLEN
FAMILY FOUNDATION

Anonymous

Jill Baker and Jeffrey Bishop

Donna and Matt Bellew

John Branch

Diana Broze

Sarah and Tim Cavanaugh

Janet and Les Cox

Mimi Gardner Gates

Linda Gerrard and Walter Parsons

Gull Industries, Inc.
on behalf of Ruth and William True

The Trust of Warren A. Gummow

Steven Myron Holl

Phil Kovacevich and Eric Wechsler

Lakeside Industries, Inc.
on behalf of Jeanne Marie Lee

TO LEARN MORE ABOUT UNDERWRITING
COPPER CANYON PRESS TITLES,
PLEASE CALL 360-385-4925 EXT. 103

WE ARE GRATEFUL FOR THE MAJOR SUPPORT PROVIDED BY:

Maureen Lee and Mark Busto

Rhoady Lee and Alan Gartenhaus

Ellie Mathews and Carl Youngmann as The North Press

Anne O'Donnell and John Phillips

Petunia Charitable Fund and advisor Elizabeth Hebert

Suzie Rapp and Mark Hamilton

Jill and Bill Ruckelshaus

Cynthia Lovelace Sears and Frank Buxton

Kim and Jeff Seely

Catherine Eaton Skinner and David Skinner

Dan Waggoner

Austin Walters

Barbara and Charles Wright

The dedicated interns and faithful volunteers
of Copper Canyon Press

The Chinese character for poetry is made up of two parts: "word" and "temple." It also serves as pressmark for Copper Canyon Press.

This book is set in Minion, designed for digital composition by Robert Slimbach. Titles are set in Fresco by Fred Smeijers. Book design and composition by VJB/Scribe. Printed on archival-quality paper using soy-based inks.